Copyright Kylie Kajewski 2023

MY FIRST DAY

Written by Kylie Kajewski
Illustrated by Emma Ruhlmann-Bleicher

Dear Parents and Carers,

Thank you for purchasing "My First Day". This book is designed for both parents and children to know what to expect and ease the anxiety of entering childcare. I worked as an Early Childhood Educator from the years 2009 until 2019, starting out as the bus driver, then as an assistant, lead educator, director and the cook. I've seen all angles of early childhood, and have three children of my own.

Childcare centres are generally very busy, noisy and active establishments. This is the first hurdle. Children who have not been exposed to this type of noise or activity will naturally have feelings of being scared or intimidated. Your second challenge is leaving your babies with strangers. If you don't feel comfortable, your child won't either. My advice for both these challenges is to make time to have short visits with your child and their room educators. Most centres will actively encourage you to do this. Ask for their "Open Door Policy" which means when your child is enrolled, you can stay for as long as you like, or at least until you and your child feel comfortable.

One of the most important things for new parents to do is reassure your child that you are coming back, and when. Not time specific because children can't tell the time. Tell them you will be back after rest time, for example. Make good-byes quick and do them once only. The longer it takes you to say good-bye, the more your child will get worked up. Let the educators do their job in this instance, you may think that the educator walking away with your child is harsh, but trust me, once you're gone they have no time to pine for you as the educators will have a day's worth of activities planned. We won't let your children cry - if they don't settle - we will call you.

When packing your child's belongings, make sure to pack any comforters they may use at home. If your child is going to be in care for more than two days a week, I would suggest having a second or back-up comforter or better yet, leaving one at the centre and not relying on remembering to pick it up in the afternoons. Educators do their best however they're only human too, and they can and will forget to pack up items at times. It is always a good idea to also name everything that goes in with your child. Imagine your two year old in a room with fourteen other two year olds all obsessed with the latest animated character. They will also all have the same or similar clothing and shoe sizes. This makes for a lot of items that can possibly be lost or mistaken as belonging to someone else.

You may also like to send in a family photo. Be sure to include as many important people or pets as possible. This is a great tool to help both your child's educator ask questions and engage with your child while also helping your child feel calm. Write a list of their names down for the educator to refer to.

Try to enroll your child for a minimum of two days a week, one day a week is not often enough to become used too. Also try to have your child dropped off and picked up at the same time each day. This sets them up in a good routine with no surprises, and you may never know exactly how much they love fruit time! Most centres will offer a variety of fresh fruits and vegetables three times a day. Your child probably won't eat what is being offered in care at home, but they will eat it while in care when they see the other children eating it.

My final piece of advice is to keep your child involved and informed. Children are smart and often understand more than we give them credit for. Talk to your child, read them this book and talk to friends and family about what their children do while in care. Take your child shopping for a new set of cot sheets (cot sheets fit childcare beds really well, and you can pick them up from the second-hand shop), buy a new backpack, hat and water bottle, but check with your centre first, as they may provide these items. Talk about how much fun they're going to have, how brave they are and how proud of them you are for trying something new. Give them time to settle in and explore. Don't be too hard on yourself or your child if it doesn't go to plan, either. Rome wasn't built in a day.

I wish you, your child and your family every success in this new, scary yet exciting time of their little lives.

Warmest regards,
🌸 Kylie Kajewski

Find out more at modernmumco.com
and on social media:

� Modern Mum & Co

� modern_mumco

We enter the yard,
where the children play and shout.
I see another child crying;
I wonder what that's about?

This place just looks so terrifying, so much activity going on.

If we turn and run now,
no one will know we've gone.

"Hello there", we hear a voice from across the yard.
This must be my educator; this part will be hard.

Mummy says hello back, and they start to chatter.

My eyes dart around the place –
Is that a fruit platter?

All the children run away; I see them wash their hands.
They all sit down with each other; they too must be fruit fans.

The educator offers me a seat, and mummy sets me down.
I don't like this at all, and I begin to frown.

Mummy kneels beside me and offers me the fruit.
"You'll have a good day" she says "I know you'll have a hoot".

She cuddles me and kisses my forehead as she says her goodbyes.
"I'll be back after your nap, with a big surprise!"

Now mummy has gone and I am left alone,
I'll wait right here for her return.

"C'mon now let's get you set,
there is SO much here to learn".

The children are laughing and having fun,
there are squeals of delight.
There's so much to choose from;
books, crafts and paints that are so bright.

This all looks very interesting, I'll see what all the fuss is.
But soon my mind turns to mummy —
"Where is mummy?" I quiz.

"Here is a photo of your mum, your dad and sister too".
"Is this your puppy and your kitty? I heard you named her Blue".

My educators seem to be nice, and they're giving me my space.
I guess it'll take a little while, to settle in this place.

We played outside and inside, we sung many nursery rhymes.
Then I heard the educators say that it was lunchtime!

Great! I'm so very hungry, I'll go wash my hands too.
Ohh, thank you for reminding me I must first use the loo.

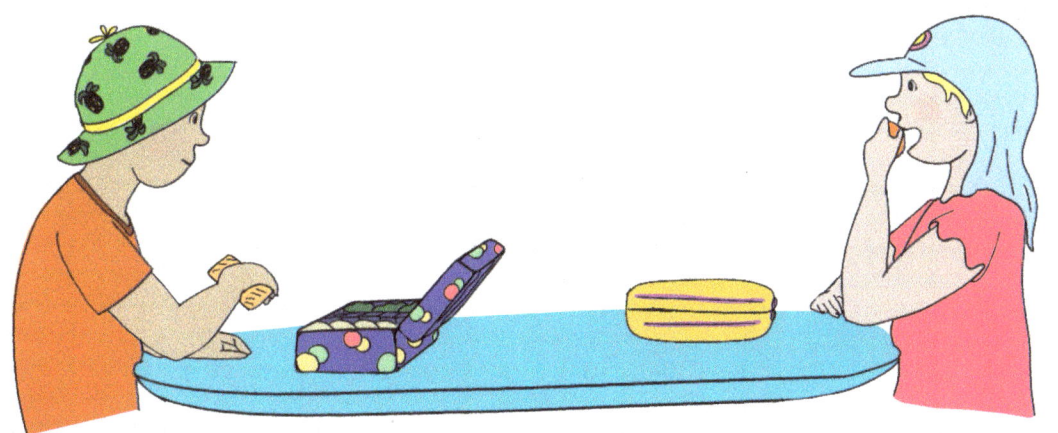

Sitting down to eat again the room goes quiet and dark.
The beds are out they're getting made, I see mummy packed my shark.

After my nap she will return and I can then go home.
I wonder what my surprise will be,
maybe she'll let me play on her phone.

The lights are on, I open my eyes there is movement all around.
I've had my nap, so I must now be homeward bound.

More food is being offered, "afternoon tea" they say.
Maybe I'll have a nibble, before I end my day.

We put our sunscreen, shoes and hat on, then we go outside.
I look around for something to do, I think I'll play on the slide.

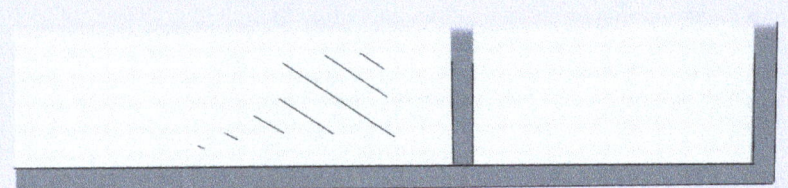

"Hello sweetheart" – I hear a familiar voice call out.
I turn to look, "It's mummy!" I shout.

Today was tough on everyone as we started something new.
Tomorrow I'll be back again and be prepared for my day two!

www.ingramcontent.com/pod-product-compliance
Lightning Source LLC
Chambersburg PA
CBHW061400160426
42811CB00099B/1297